W9-ARK-408

THE

HOME DISTILLER'S HAND BOOK

Make Your Own Whiskey & Bourbon Blends, Infused Spirits & Cordials

MATTHEW TEACHER

CIDER MILL
PRESS

BOOK
PUBLISHERS

Kennebunkport, Maine

Cider Mill Press Book Publishers
"Where good books are ready for press"
12 Port Farm Road
Kennebunkport, Maine 04046

Visit us on the Web!
www.cidermillpress.com

Design by Alicia Freile, Tango Media Pty Ltd
Typography: NeutraText, Rosewood, Bodoni Ornaments, and Adobe Caslon
Photographs by Kitchen Konfidence Photography
Printed in China

4 5 6 7 8 9 0

CONTENTS

INTRODUCTION

Are you the kind of person who goes "off recipe" when cooking a big meal? Do you ever sit with a glass of bourbon mentally devising the different ways you can take this wonderful drink and make it even better? If you're a risk-taker who likes to dabble, invent, experiment, and concoct (especially when it comes to your alcoholic beverages), you've come to the right place! This book guides you step-by-step through the process of creating unique and delicious alcoholic infusions and blends as well as infused cordials and crèmes—all with simple ingredients and all within the confines of your home. You don't need a special degree or fancy equipment, just this book and a propensity for trying something new.

Blended? Infused? Confused?

So, just what am I talking about here? Well, first off, we won't actually be making any alcohol from scratch. (Without a license it's illegal.) However, it's perfectly okay (more or less) to take store-bought alcohol and add to it a variety of herbs, spices, fruits, and more, hence creating your own custom-flavored drink. The collection of amazing infusions included in this book is sure to make your mouth water with anticipation and impress all your friends and family.

In these pages you will find a how-to guide for blending and infusing, amazing recipes from some of today's leading mixologists, safety and legal information, a reference section, inspiring quotations, and much more. *The Home Distiller's Handbook* is all you need to know to go from beginner to pro mixologist in no time at all!

What's the difference between infusing and blending?

Infusion is the addition of herbs, spices, etc. to store-bought alcohol. Blending is the process of taking two or more store-bought whiskies and blending them together, creating a custom flavor.

Your body is a temple.
Fill it with spirits.

— UNKNOWN

THE LAW

❀ You are not allowed by law to distill your own alcohol from scratch. All infusions and blends must be created with existing spirits.

❀ You are not allowed to sell the blends and infusions you create. Homemade spirits and blends will make terrific gifts and party favors, though.

❀ This book contains many resources and makes various recommendations, not all of which are legal in all areas of the United States and abroad. Please take it upon yourself to know the laws in your region.

ABC Crackdown in San Francisco

Recently, one of the hotbeds of infusions has been San Francisco. Some truly innovative creations were being offered at numerous bars in the area. The ABC, or the Alcoholic Beverage Commission, in California has ruled that bars making their own infusions are in fact breaking the law by altering liquor and selling it. Bars have been required to stop infusing. If you live in California, please contact your representative to put an end to this crackdown.

SAFETY

❀ When making cordials and crèmes, do not add sugar to any liquor with less than 18 percent alcohol. The yeast will eat up the sugar creating carbon dioxide. This creates carbonation and can cause the bottles to explode.

❀ Be aware of the containers you use for making your infusions. You do not want to use plastic bottles or jugs or old leaded crystal jars as they can transfer their chemical taste into your liquid. These containers can impart an unpleasant taste into your infusion and even dangerous chemicals (especially with the lead). Also, do not use any containers that have stored anything except other liquors or foods, as residue can corrupt the purity of the taste.

❀ Refrigerate any liqueurs or crèmes you make that contain dairy products.

INFUSIONS

What separates a mixologist from a bartender? The answer is: a lot more than you think. Bartenders are master mixers of existing drinks, while mixologists concoct *original* cocktails with precise ratios, blending flavors to excite the imbiber's pallet in unique and stimulating ways.

The revival of handcrafted cocktails has created a boom in creativity. One of the most commanding tools a mixologist has is the power of infusion (also known as *maceration*). With it, you have the power to combine the essence of a habanero pepper into tequila, the know-how to extract the taste of a fresh orange into your vodka, and the creativity to combine your whiskey with smoky bacon. For the first time, the following collection of infusions, highlighted with creations from some of the world's leading mixologists, can be yours to create in the comfort of your own home.

MAKING AN INFUSION

You can infuse any type of liquor, from low alcohol content cordials and crèmes to high alcohol content vodka, whiskey, tequila, gin and more. The first step in this process is to choose your liquor. Keep in mind the alcohol's original quality and pick something that will complement it. Rum is spicy, gin has a floral aroma, vodka is an open pallet, and whiskey can be smoky and sweet. I recommend choosing good quality liquors with tastes you already enjoy.

After you've chosen your combination, gather these items and you'll be ready to go:

1. Your liquor choice
2. Your infusion ingredient(s)
3. A glass bottle or infusion jar with a stopper
4. A strainer, coffee filters, or cheesecloth
5. A funnel

Upon gathering your materials follow these instructions:

1. Prep and clean your ingredients. If you're using jalapeños as your ingredient, you should wash them. Depending on the amount of spice you wish to add, you can leave them whole or slice them open for more intensity. This is also true for garlic.
2. Make sure your infusion jar is clean and dry.
3. Place your ingredients in the jar.

4. Pour the alcohol into the jar using a funnel, making sure to submerge your ingredients.
5. Seal the jar with the stopper or lid.
6. Give the jar a good shake.
7. Store the jar in a cool place out of direct sunlight for steeping. You will want to gently shake or stir the jar daily to recombine the ingredients.
8. Taste daily.
9. When your infusion is ready to be bottled, strain the infusion ingredients, using a funnel lined with coffee filters or cheesecloth, and you're good to go.

The infusion process can take anywhere from three days to a month. It depends on what ingredients you are using and personal taste. A general tip is that more intense ingredients such as jalapeños, garlic, and citrus fruit will infuse in three to five days, while more subtle choices such as herbs or berries can steep for a week or longer. Taste the infused liquor every day to check in on its progress. When the essence of your ingredient shines through, but is not overpowering, it's ready.

To purchase infusion jars and other supplies see the Resources & Supplies section on page 138.

INFUSION TIPS

🏵 Vodka is the most neutral liquor. It can be infused with many different ingredients.

🏵 Try to use vodka that has been distilled at least three times as it's a clearer and purer palette.

🏵 Time equals intensity when it comes to infusion.

🏵 When infusing citrus fruits, much of their flavor comes from the zest or peel. Use a zester or vegetable peeler to remove just the zest. Do not include the white inner peel as it infuses a bitter quality.

🏵 Use fresh, local ingredients. If they taste better when eaten, they'll make a better tasting infusion.

MOST DISTILLERS choose not to rotate their barrels. Not us. We like ours to get out and move around. And by move around, we mean rotate. It ensures every barrel experiences the same aging process. And you know what they say: a moving barrel gathers no moss.

— MAKER'S MARK

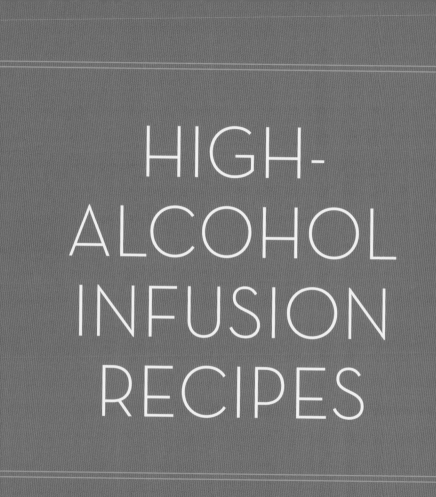

HIGH-ALCOHOL INFUSION RECIPES

Here are some classic combinations to get you started.

GRAPEFRUIT RUM

The grapefruit essence lends itself to warm summer nights, and it pairs with seafood as well as avocado and carrots. It's great for celebrating in the Caribbean or bringing the tropical sun into your winter-worn home.

750 ml rum

1 large pink grapefruit

1. Slice the grapefruit and remove the peel.
2. Place sliced grapefruit in bottom of infusion jar.
3. Add rum and seal the jar.
4. Let infuse for 1-2 weeks out of direct sunlight, tasting and gently shaking regularly.
5. Strain the rum into a clean bottle and cap.

TIP

You may also include the zest from the grapefruit peel. Just be sure to only use the outer layer of the peel and not the white portion.

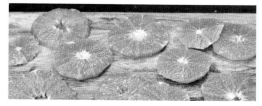

COCONUT RUM

Coconut rum is great for all things beach related. This is sure to spruce up a Piña Colada or a Hurricane. It pairs well with Thai and Caribbean food.

750 ml white rum

1 coconut

1. Drill a hole in the coconut, drain and discard the liquid.
2. Break up coconut into pieces and peel off shell.
3. Place coconut pieces in a food processor and shred.
4. Place shredded coconut in bottom of infusion jar.
5. Add rum and seal the jar.
6. Let infuse for 2 weeks out of direct sunlight, tasting and gently shaking regularly.
7. Strain the rum into a clean bottle and cap.

PEAR APPLE RUM

Having a party and need an exciting new cocktail to serve? Many great libations are at your fingertips with pear apple rum on hand. Try a spiced pear Appletini, which is sure impress guests' palates! All you need to do is mix infused rum, simple syrup (see page 61), fresh cinnamon, and limejuice for a beverage that perfectly captures the essence of early fall.

750 ml rum

1 large red pear

4 red apples

1. Wash apples and pear.
2. Slice apples and pear into eighths.
3. Place sliced apples and pear in bottom of infusion jar.
4. Add rum and seal the jar.
5. Let infuse for 1-2 weeks out of direct sunlight, tasting and gently shaking regularly.
6. Strain the rum into a clean bottle and cap.

CHERRY VODKA

Steeping cherries in vodka is a surefire way to add some sweetness and tartness to your vodka cocktails. Try it in a Cosmopolitan or Cherry Martini (with an alcoholic cherry as the garnish).

750 ml vodka

8 cups cherries

1. Wash cherries.

2. Remove the stems and pit the cherries.

3. Place cherries in bottom of infusion jar.

4. Add vodka and seal the jar.

5. Let infuse for 5-7 days out of direct sunlight, tasting and gently shaking regularly until desired intensity is reached.

6. Strain the vodka into a clean bottle, cap, and refrigerate.

TIP

The vodka soaked cherries can make an excellent cocktail garnish.

> In the United States, cherries are the freshest (and tastiest) in the summer months—from May to August.

Worthless people live only to eat and drink;
people of worth eat and drink only to live.

— SOCRATES

THINK OF the exercise (speaking of home vatting) as painting onto a canvas (a common analogy cited by professional blenders), with the core malt representing the "canvas" and those smaller amounts of the additional malts being the "colouring."

— DOUG KUEBLER, *CIGAR WEEKLY*

JALAPEÑO PEPPER VODKA

Ready for some spice? This vodka is great for Sunday morning brunch Bloody Marys and a surefire cure for the weekend hangover.

750 ml vodka

1-2 fresh jalapeño peppers

1. Wash jalapeño peppers.
2. Place whole peppers in bottom of infusion jar.
3. Add vodka and seal the jar.
4. Let infuse for 1-4 days out of direct sunlight, tasting and gently shaking regularly until desired intensity is reached.
5. Strain the vodka into a clean bottle, cap, and refrigerate.

TIP

If you want a more intense heat and spice, cut and deseed the peppers before infusing. The infusion time really depends on how spicy you want your vodka to be.

SUMMERTIME WATERMELON VODKA

Having a pool party this summer? Make some watermelon infused vodka ahead of time and then create a refreshing poolside punch for your guests. The sweet character of this infusion is also a hit in vodka martinis and gimlets. Garnish with a fresh slice of watermelon for an aesthetic masterpiece.

750 ml vodka

1 watermelon

1. Slice approximately ⅛th of a large watermelon into cubes. Do not include the rind.
2. Place cubed watermelon in bottom of infusion jar.
3. Add vodka, covering the watermelon cubes, and seal the jar.
4. Let infuse for 5-7 days out of direct sunlight, tasting and gently shaking regularly.
5. Strain the vodka into a clean bottle, cap and refrigerate.

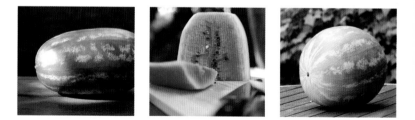

CUCUMBER VODKA

This subtle yet revitalizing infusion yields a cool, crisp libation. Make a batch of martinis, cosmos, or gimlets and pair with sushi or other fresh seafood.

750 ml vodka

1½ cups cucumber

1. Wash, peel, and slice 1½ cups of cucumbers.

2. Place sliced cucumber in bottom of infusion jar.

3. Add vodka, covering the cucumber, and seal the jar.

4. Let infuse for 1-2 weeks out of direct sunlight, tasting and gently shaking regularly.

5. Strain the vodka into a clean bottle, cap, and refrigerate.

Glassware

- **BrandySnifter:** Many drinkers use a brandy snifter when drinking their bourbon neat. The snifter has a unique shape that keeps the aroma in the glass and provides an enjoyable sensory experience.

- **Cocktail glass:** A long-stemmed glass with a triangular bowl, often used for martinis, gimlets, Manhattans, and other cocktails all served straight-up (without ice).

- **Cordial glass:** A short-stemmed glass used for serving small amounts of sweet cordials.

- **Hghball glass:** A glass with straight sides often used for cocktails on the rocks.

PUMPKIN VODKA

While the kids are out in search of candy, sit down with a few friends and enjoy a grown-up Halloween with a Pumpkin Martini. If your little ones (if you have little ones) are in need of a chaperone, this infusion will warm up your bones before a brisk fall evening walk.

750 ml of vodka

1 pumpkin (you won't use the whole thing)

1. Wash pumpkin.
2. Use a vegetable peeler to shave 12 thin ribbons (each approximately 6 inches in length) off the pumpkin.
3. Place pumpkin ribbons in bottom of infusion jar.
4. Add the vodka and seal the jar.
5. Let infuse for 1-2 weeks out of direct sunlight, tasting and gently shaking regularly until desired intensity is reached.
6. Strain the vodka into a clean bottle, cap, and refrigerate.

TIP

Add 5 or so cloves in the second week to step it up a notch.

CANDY CORN VODKA

This Halloween favorite might look appealing to youngsters, so make sure you set aside a secondary bowl of candy corn for *their* consumption. An example of the new fad of candy-infused alcohol, this vodka makes for a great dessert cocktail. Depending on infusion time, your infused vodka should have a bright, irresistible color and sweet taste to match.

750 ml vodka

3 cups candy corn

1. Place candy corn in bottom of infusion jar.
2. Add vodka and seal the jar.
3. Let infuse for 2-5 days or more out of direct sunlight, tasting and gently shaking regularly.
4. Strain the vodka into a clean bottle, cap, and refrigerate.

TIP

Try using this infusion in a candy corn martini.

There are lots of candies you can infuse with, such as jellybeans.

VANILLA VODKA

Want to be prepared to impress those unexpected guests? Vanilla Vodka is a great all-purpose infusion to have kicking around. Use it for White or Black Russians, martinis, or a Screwdriver.

750 ml vodka

2 whole vanilla beans

1. Wash vanilla beans.
2. Slice both beans open but not in half.
3. Place vanilla beans in bottom of infusion jar.
4. Add vodka, covering the beans, and seal the jar.
5. Let infuse for 1-2 weeks out of direct sunlight, tasting and gently shaking regularly.
6. Strain the vodka into a clean bottle, cap, and refrigerate.

RASPBERRY VODKA

Raspberry Vodka's fresh redolent quality complements a variety of cocktails. Try serving Raspberry Vodka Martinis at Sunday brunch. You may be surprised how good a raspberry Bloody Mary can be. Sounds a little off, but don't judge until you've tried.

750 ml vodka

⅔ cup raspberries

1. Wash raspberries.
2. Place raspberries in bottom of infusion jar.
3. Add vodka, covering the raspberries, and seal the jar.
4. Let infuse for 1-2 weeks out of direct sunlight, tasting and gently shaking regularly.
5. Strain the vodka into a clean bottle, cap, and refrigerate.

EARL GREY GIN

A mild Earl Grey infusion can be well suited for many cocktails. The Earl Grey will impart a refreshing earthy tone that complements the gin's juniper and coriander zest. Impress your friends with your custom Earl Grey Gin and Tonic with a sprig of fresh mint at a spring gathering.

1 liter of gin

¼ cup of loose Earl Grey tea leaves

1. Place loose tea leaves in bottom of infusion jar.
2. Add gin, covering the tea leaves, and seal the jar.
3. Let infuse for approximately 2 hours out of direct sunlight.
4. Strain the gin into a clean bottle, cap, and refrigerate.

TIP

Tea infuses quickly, so keep an eye on it.

RASPBERRY GIN

This summertime infusion goes great with an outdoor picnic or for sitting by the pool. Whip up a Negroni, a Gin Fizz, or your favorite summertime cocktail, and step into the sun!

750 ml gin

⅔ cup raspberries

1. Wash raspberries.
2. Place raspberries in bottom of infusion jar.
3. Add gin, covering the raspberries, and seal the jar.
4. Let infuse for 1-2 weeks out of direct sunlight, tasting and gently shaking regularly.
5. Strain the gin into a clean bottle, cap, and refrigerate.

IT IS WELL to remember that there are five reasons for drinking: the arrival of a friend, one's present or future thirst, the excellence of the wine, or any other reason.

— LATIN PROVERB

CUCUMBER GIN

The cucumber infused gin is great in a martini, a Gibson, or the lesser known, Gin Rickey (typically made with bourbon). For any of these drinks, use chilled, fresh cucumber slices as a garnish. Try out this infusion with a seafood dinner.

750 ml gin

1½ cups cucumber

1. Wash, peel, and slice 1½ cups of cucumbers.
2. Place sliced cucumber in bottom of infusion jar.
3. Add gin, covering the cucumber, and seal the jar.
4. Let infuse for 1-2 weeks out of direct sunlight, tasting and gently shaking regularly.
5. Strain the gin into a clean bottle, cap, and refrigerate.

SMOKED BACON BOURBON

This infusion is good for sipping by the fire after a big dinner. If drinking neat or with whiskey stones, add one or two drops of water before sipping. This will open up the bourbon's aromatic nature. It's also flavorsome chilled with an ice cube or two.

750 ml bourbon

3-4 strips of smoky bacon (30 ml bacon fat)

1. Fully cook 4 strips of bacon in a pan.
2. Remove the bacon from the pan (eat or discard).
3. Let the bacon fat cool but not solidify.
4. Measure out 30 ml of rendered bacon fat.
5. Pour bacon fat into infusion jar.
6. Add bourbon and seal the jar.

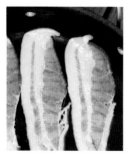

7. Let infuse for between 1-2 days or more, out of direct sunlight, gently shaking regularly.

8. After desired taste is achieved, place in freezer overnight. This will cause the fat to congeal and separate from the alcohol, making it easy to strain.

9. Strain the whiskey into a clean bottle and cap.

TIP

Use smoky bacon to really get the flavor and aroma infused into your whiskey. You may also include the actual strips of bacon in the infusion.

Spelling Lesson

Both *whisky* and *whiskey* are accepted spellings. *Whisky* is of Scottish heritage and still used today while *Whiskey* is used by most American distilleries. There are exceptions such as Maker's Mark bourbon, which does not include the "e."

Ice Shapes and Melting

● Most people don't give a second thought to what shape their ice is as they fill their glass. But, if you want to keep your whiskey cold without diluting it, the sphere is the shape for you. Of all shapes, a sphere has the smallest surface area for a volume. This means that the ice melts slower, keeping your drink cold and not too diluted.

● Stop polluting your whiskey with chlorine. Either filter your water or use spring water for your ice cubes.

● You can use unusual items to make larger ice cubes than you would with a standard tray.

BLUEBERRY BOURBON

Blueberries and bourbon … who would have thought? This infusion makes a surprisingly good Manhattan or Mint Julep on a warm summer's eve. Many find it appealing over ice cream as well.

1 liter bourbon

⅔ cup blueberries

1. Wash blueberries.
2. Place blueberries in bottom of infusion jar.
3. Slightly muddle blueberries—break them slightly open, but leave them whole.
4. Add bourbon and seal the jar.
5. Let infuse for 2-5 days out of direct sunlight, tasting and gently shaking daily.
6. Strain the bourbon into a clean bottle and cap.

CHERRY WHISKEY

The cherry essence imparts sweet and tart components to a quality whiskey. The degree is dependant upon the type of cherries used and infusion time. It makes beautiful Manhattans and the infused cherries not only look great as a garnish, but also pack a punch. Might be wise to limit one cherry per person (or at least one per drink).

750 ml whiskey

8 cups cherries

1. Wash, stem, and pit the cherries.
2. Place cherries in bottom of infusion jar.
3. Add whiskey, covering the cherries, and seal the jar.
4. Let infuse for 2-7 days out of direct sunlight, tasting and gently shaking regularly until desired intensity is reached.
5. Strain the whiskey into a clean bottle, cap, and refrigerate.

Adding Water to Cocktails

Adding a little spring water to your whiskey can actually enhance the aroma while cutting some of the burn. Aroma molecules evaporate a good deal better in water than alcohol. This is because aroma molecules are closer chemically to alcohol. Add a little water and take a smell. This applies to anything with high alcohol content, including wines.

I decided to stop drinking with creeps.
I decided to drink only with friends.
I've lost thirty pounds.

—ERNEST HEMINGWAY

HABANERO PEPPER TEQUILA

This one packs a punch. After your infusion has reached the desired spice intensity, rack or strain the liquor and concoct some spicy margaritas. For the extremely brave, a fresh habanero ring may be used as a garnish. Goes great with a burger and fries.

750 ml tequila

3 habanero peppers

1. Wash habanero peppers.
2. Slice pepper tops off, and cut in half lengthwise.
3. Remove all seeds, but leave the ribbing.
4. Place the halved peppers in bottom of infusion jar.

5. Add tequila and seal the jar.

6. Let infuse for 3 days or more in a cool place out of direct sunlight, tasting and gently shaking regularly until desired intensity is reached.

7. Strain the tequila into a clean bottle and cap.

TIP

Do not leave the pepper seeds in. They will overpower the whole infusion. If you'd like more spice, add another seeded pepper.

A dash of peat or salt can both embellish and help to bind together a blend.

— DOUG KUEBLER, *CIGAR WEEKLY*

PINEAPPLE TEQUILA

Can you feel the warm sun on your face as you imbibe the first taste of your new pineapple tequila infusion? This was made for frozen margaritas on a warm sunny day. Pair with fresh seafood such as shrimp or scallops.

750 ml tequila

1 pineapple

1. Slice the pineapple into rings.
2. Place pineapple rings in bottom of infusion jar.
3. Add tequila, covering the pineapple, and seal the jar.
4. Let infuse for 1-2 weeks out of direct sunlight, tasting and gently shaking regularly.
5. Strain the tequila into a clean bottle, cap, and refrigerate.

SILVER KIWI STRAWBERRY TEQUILA

Kiwi Strawberry Tequila adds a summery nectarous essence to your favorite tequila cocktail. Margaritas by the pool … Tequila Sunrise in a hammock … a nice cold punch under the sun….

750 ml silver tequila

3-4 cups fresh strawberries

1 kiwi

1. Slice kiwi and remove the peel.
2. Wash and slice strawberries.
3. Place sliced kiwi and strawberries in bottom of infusion jar.
4. Add tequila and seal the jar.
5. Let infuse for 2-3 weeks out of direct sunlight, tasting and gently shaking regularly.
6. Strain the tequila into a clean bottle, cap, and refrigerate.

WALNUT COGNAC

Walnut Cognac is the glass you want by your side on a cold winter's night. Try sipping this neat (no ice) out of a snifter. The toasty nutty flavor complements a sweet desert or a nice cigar.

750 ml cognac

2 cups shelled walnuts

1. Shell walnuts.
2. Toast walnuts in the oven for 15 minutes at 400°F on a baking sheet.
3. Place walnuts in bottom of infusion jar.
4. Add cognac and seal the jar.
5. Let infuse for 5-7 days out of direct sunlight, tasting and gently shaking regularly.
6. Strain the cognac into a clean bottle and cap.

LOW-
ALCOHOL
INFUSION
RECIPES

Cordials and crèmes are infusions that generally contain a smaller amount of alcohol (17-30 percent) and are sweeter, due to the addition of simple syrup or other sweeteners. When making liqueurs, many find it is best to use as neutral a palette as possible. Although not available in all states, the best choice for a neutral alcoholic base is high-proof grain alcohol.

If pure grain alcohol is not available in your state, the next best choice is non-flavored vodka. In the United States, all non-flavored vodka is legally required to be odorless, colorless, and tasteless. If you're interested in showcasing the pure essence of your ingredients, this is the best choice. Although not as widely used, other choices for your alcoholic base are brandy, rum, whiskey, and gin.

After you have chosen your alcoholic base, choose your fruits, nuts, herbs, spices, or flavored extracts.

Although most cordials and crèmes are made with simple syrup (made from sucrose or table sugar), there are other options to consider based on your desired outcome. Some other options include: honey, brown sugar, or corn syrup, all of which have a distinctive flavor. Simple syrup does not impart any flavor to your infusion, so if you opt for another sweetener, know that it will affect the taste of your end result.

How to Make Simple Syrup

1. Combine equal parts sugar and water in a saucepan.
2. Bring to a boil over medium-high heat.
3. Stir continuously until all the sugar has dissolved and the liquid is clear. Make sure not to burn the sugar.
4. Remove from heat and store in a container for future use.

Note: Experiment with the ratio of water to sugar. For some infusions, thicker simple syrup may be more desirable.

Candy is dandy but liquor is quicker.

— OGDEN NASH

PINEAPPLE BASIL CORDIAL

This refreshing cordial complements any lazy summer day by the pool. It's also fantastic for entertaining friends and family for brunch. Pair with a light fare menu of quiche, fresh fruit, and finger sandwiches. This cordial combines the tropical fruit with the fresh herbs of a summertime garden.

750 ml grain alcohol or non-flavored vodka

1 pineapple

3 tablespoons fresh chopped basil

1. Slice the pineapple into rings.

2. Chop basil.

3. Combine pineapple and basil in bottom of infusion jar.

4. Pour in alcohol, covering pineapple and basil, and seal the jar tightly.

5. Let infuse for 30 days or more in a cool place out of direct sunlight, tasting and remixing daily until desired intensity is reached.

6. Strain or rack the cordial into a clean bottle.

7. Add simple syrup to taste and tightly cap.

8. Let it rest out of direct sunlight for at least 30 days, preferably a year or more.

Note: You can also add a small amount of pineapple juice to this infusion.

You can use ordinary kitchen skewers to build a "tower of pineapple slices" within the jar. To do this, evenly space your pineapple slices on four or more skewers so it makes a tower. Then stand the tower vertically in the infusion jar. Having the pineapple spaced out will release more of its flavor into your liquor.

Racking vs. Straining

For cordials and crèmes you may prefer to use the racking method to filter out the fruits, nuts, herbs, and spices. Filtering through coffee filters or cheesecloth can take a long time with thicker liquors.

What You Need
● Approximately 3 feet of clear plastic tubing (you can find it at any pet supply store sold for aquariums)
● Matured infusion in original jar
● An additional infusion jar or suitable container

What You Do
1. Place the jar containing the matured infusion on an elevated surface.
2. Place the second clean jar on a surface that is lower than the first jar. (The kitchen sink or bathtub works well).
3. Feed one end of the plastic tubing into the jar containing the liqueur until it's 1 or 2 inches from the settled ingredients at the bottom. (Do not disturb the sediment at the bottom of the jar.)
4. Suck on the other end of the tube, like a straw, to get the liquid flowing, and then place it in the second lower jar.
5. The liquid will flow through the tube into the clean jar, leaving the solids in the original jar.

STRAWBERRY ROSEMARY CORDIAL

Summer in a bottle! Let the sun sparkle off the beautiful red and pink hues of this sweet berry-and-garden inspired beverage. Share a glass or two with a loved one on the front porch or deck: garnish with fresh berries or a sprig of mint.

750 ml white brandy

5 cups chopped fresh strawberries

5 sprigs fresh rosemary

1. Wash, stem, and halve strawberries.
2. Place strawberries in bottom of infusion jar.
3. Pour in brandy, covering the strawberries.
4. Place rosemary into alcohol, submerging the strawberries, and seal the jar tightly.
5. Let infuse for 1-3 months or more in a cool place out of direct sunlight, tasting and remixing daily until desired intensity is reached.
6. Strain or rack the cordial into a clean bottle.
7. Add simple syrup to taste and tightly cap.
8. Let it rest out of direct sunlight for at least 30 days, preferably a year or more.

OCTOBER APPLE LIQUEUR

As the leaves are exploding with color and the air turns crisp and cold, warm up your friends and family with the quintessential essence of fall: fresh apples. Have a glass after raking the leaves or drizzle over pound cake for an autumn-inspired dessert.

500 ml grain alcohol or non-flavored vodka

250 ml brandy

2½ pounds fresh apples

3 cinnamon sticks

1. Wash, stem, and slice apples in eighths.
2. Place apples and cinnamon sticks in bottom of infusion jar.
3. Pour in grain alcohol or vodka and brandy, covering the apples and cinnamon sticks, and seal the jar tightly.
4. Let infuse for 1-2 months in a cool place out of direct sunlight, tasting and gently shaking daily until desired intensity is reached.

5. Strain or rack the cordial into a clean bottle.

6. Add simple syrup to taste and cap tightly.

7. Let it rest out of direct sunlight for at least 30 days, preferably a year or more.

TIP

After straining your apples from the liqueur, place apples in a large re-sealable bag and crush to release the absorbed alcohol. Then filter out small apple pieces through a fine cheesecloth and pour liquid back into the liqueur with the simple syrup.

There can't be good living where
there is not good drinking.

— BENJAMIN FRANKLIN

PISTACHIO LIQUEUR

Celebrating life with a family-style Italian feast? Serve this nutty liqueur after dinner to complement a dark chocolate dessert. Sip slowly and enjoy this smooth and rich digestif.

500 ml grain alcohol or non-flavored vodka

1 teaspoon pistachio extract flavoring

1 teaspoon glycerin

Food coloring (optional)

250 ml simple syrup

1. Combine grain alcohol or vodka, and pistachio extract in an infusion jar.
2. Add glycerin and food coloring to simple syrup.
3. Pour simple syrup mix into infusion jar, stir and cap tightly.
4. Let it infuse for 1-2 months in a cool place out of direct sunlight, tasting and gently shaking regularly until desired intensity is reached.

TIP

Adding glycerin to your cordial will thicken it.

PRUNE LIQUEUR

Get the party moving with this fruit-infused spirit! Sip this delicious beverage, use it for cooking, or pair with a ricotta cheesecake for a spectacular dessert.

500 ml grain alcohol or non-flavored vodka

250 ml brandy

1 pound dried pitted prunes

TIP

Many infusionists add food coloring to achieve a desired color.

1. Chop prunes into quarters.
2. Place prunes in bottom of infusion jar.
3. Pour in grain alcohol or vodka and brandy, covering the prunes, and seal the jar tightly.
4. Let infuse for 2-3 months in a cool place out of direct sunlight, tasting and gently shaking daily until desired intensity is reached.
5. Strain or rack the liquid into a clean bottle.
6. Add simple syrup to taste and cap tightly.
7. Let it rest out of direct sunlight for at least 30 days, preferably a year or more.

BLACKBERRY HONEY BRANDY CORDIAL

Time to light a few candles and put on your favorite jazz record!
Relax fireside with a glass and share a slow dance with your partner.
Don't be afraid to drizzle this cordial over some homemade vanilla
ice cream!

750 ml brandy

4 cups fresh blackberries

Honey or simple syrup

1. Wash blackberries.

2. Place blackberries in bottom of infusion jar and
   muddle slightly by pressing on them so they open
   but do not split completely in half.

3. Pour in brandy, covering the blackberries, and seal
   the jar tightly.

4. Let infuse for 1 week in a cool place out of direct sunlight, tasting and gently shaking daily until desired intensity is reached.

5. Strain or rack the liquid into a clean bottle.

6. Add honey or simple syrup to taste, stir, and cap tightly.

7. Let it steep for one week or longer.

When I sell liquor, it's called bootlegging; when my patrons serve it on Lake Shore Drive, it's called hospitality.

— AL CAPONE

PLUM LIQUEUR

Serve this liqueur alone, on the rocks, or bottle it up as a lovely holiday gift. Pairs well with dark chocolate, black tea, grapes, and raspberries for an after-dinner treat.

500 ml grain alcohol or non-flavored vodka

250 ml brandy

3 pounds Damson plums

Sugar, to coat plums

Simple sugar

TIP

You may add 1 cup of water if needed while mixing the sliced plums and sugar.

1. Wash, stem, and slice plums in eighths.

2. In a mixing bowl, combine plums and sugar and mix until sugar is dissolved.

3. Place plums in bottom of infusion jar.

4. Pour in grain alcohol or vodka and brandy, covering the plums, and seal the jar tightly.

5. Let infuse for 3 months in a cool place out of direct sunlight, tasting and gently shaking daily until desired intensity is reached.

6. Strain or rack the liquid into a clean bottle.

7. After straining plums from the liqueur, place plums in a large re-sealable bag and crush to release the absorbed liquid. Then filter out small plum pieces through a cheesecloth and pour liquid back into the liqueur.

8. Add simple syrup to taste, stir, and cap tightly.

9. Let it rest out of direct sunlight for at least 30 days.

LAVENDER LIQUEUR

Dreaming of simpler, more relaxed times? Let this lavender-infused liqueur bring you back to peaceful, simpler days. Garnish with mint, serve ice cold, or add sweet rose petals or honey for the perfect afternoon luncheon.

750 ml grain alcohol or non-flavored vodka

6 tablespoons dried lavender pedals

1 cup simple syrup

1. Place dried lavender pedals in bottom of infusion jar.
2. Pour in grain alcohol or vodka, covering the pedals, and seal the jar tightly.
3. Let infuse for 1 week or more in a cool place, tasting and gently shaking daily until desired intensity is reached.
4. Strain or rack the liquid into a clean bottle.
5. Add simple syrup, stir, and cap tightly.
6. Let it rest out of direct sunlight for an additional week or two.

KAHLÚA CRÈME

Spruce up your coffee this morning with Kahlúa Crème as an alcoholic alternative to boring old milk. This crème is also delicious served over ice or drizzled atop ice cream. This is a favorite to bottle up for spectacular holiday gifts. Who doesn't love the taste of homemade Kahlúa?

750 ml grain alcohol or non-flavored vodka

16-18 cups water

6 teaspoons strong dry instant coffee

2 pounds light brown sugar

5 teaspoons vanilla extract

1. Combine water and coffee in a large pot on the stove and bring to a boil.

2. Reduce heat to low.

3. Gradually add brown sugar and bring back to a boil while stirring continuously.

4. Turn off heat and allow to cool completely. Throw in a few ice cubes to speed this process up.

5. Add vanilla extract and grain alcohol or vodka and mix well.

6. Funnel into clean bottle and cap tightly. You may serve right away, but the taste does mature well.

TIP

You may use dark brown sugar for a richer molasses taste.

Man, being reasonable, must get drunk;
the best of life is but intoxication.

— LORD BYRON

JAMES BOND: I never have more than one drink before dinner. But I do like that one to be large and very strong and very cold and very well made. This drink is my own invention. I'm going to patent it when I can think of a good name.

— IAN FLEMING, *CASINO ROYALE*

BOURBON & WHISKEY BLENDS

The making of home whiskey and bourbon blends (*home vatting*) is the process of taking two or more store-bought, single-malt whiskies and blending them together to create a custom flavor suited to your palette. Experimenting with the blending process will allow you to really get a sense of each whiskey's characteristics and how they interact. Don't ever dispose of a whiskey that you feel is not suited to your palette. These may still add a positive characteristic to a blend, and you won't end up wasting a bottle.

For the first time, start by choosing two whiskies that have unique and different characteristics. In subsequent blends, don't be afraid to try combining as many different whiskies as your taste buds desire. You may not always like the result, but no risk, no reward.

Initially choose one primary whiskey whose flavor you enjoy and add a smaller percentage of a whiskey that has a distinct characteristic. Maybe you have a lower end whiskey that is too smoky or spicy for your taste but might add complexity when blended with another single malt you enjoy. Adding a smaller portion of that to a whiskey lacking that characteristic can produce desired results. Start with a conservative portion of the lesser whiskey. You can always add more later.

Don't forget to log your blends. Keep a notebook with the whiskeys, ratios, and maturations times you've tried. Log each single malts alcohol content and calculate your finished blends alcohol by volume content as well. This will help you to refine your blends and figure out what you most enjoy.

American Whiskey

American whiskey is divided into six main categories: Bourbon, Tennessee, Rye, Corn, Wheat, and Blends. See the glossary for each alcohol's detailed attributes.

Bourbon does for me what the piece
of cake did for Proust.

— WALKER PERCY

MAKING A WHISKEY BLEND

After you've chosen two or more single malts, gather these items and you'll be ready to start.

1 bottle each of two or more brands of single-malt whiskey

2 glass decanters (at least 750 ml) with tight-fitting stoppers (you may also use clean whiskey bottles)

Measuring cup

Calculator

1. Log single malt names, alcohol by volume content, and chosen ratios.
2. Measure desired proportions of each whiskey and combine in clean glass jar.
3. Seal jar and store out of direct sunlight for maturation, tasting regularly. The vatting process can last anywhere from a few days to years.
4. Transfer the matured blend into the clean jar and seal tightly. The blend is ready to be served.

TIP

You may use an oak barrel instead of glass jars to mature your blends. This gives the vatter another tool to instill flavor. Many professional distilleries rotate their barrels throughout the vatting process to keep the blends consistent and mixed well.

Taste Along the Way

It is a good idea to get an extra glass jar to pour a small amount of your blend into for initial and intermediate tasting without opening the main bottle. This will serve as a good way to evaluate how your blend is maturing. Tasting the blend along the way will allow you to get a feel as to the balance of the vat, but keep in mind that when you taste it initially, it takes time for the two flavors to join and mature into a blend.

Consistency in Whiskey Blending

One useful tool to keep your blends consistent from one batch to the next is to leave a percentage of the previous batch in the barrel to blend with the new batch.

List of American Single Malt Whiskeys

Hudson Single Malt Whiskey

Tuthilltown Spirits

Charbay

McCarthy's

Notch

Peregrine Rock

St. George

RoughStock

Stranahan's

Wasmund's

Woodstone Creek

Gold Buckle Club - The Ellensburg Distillery

Zeppelin Bend

Bourbon Distilleries

Barton	Jim Beam	Bernheim
Four Roses	Old Rip VanWinkle	Labrot and Graham
Buffalotrace	Heaven Hill	Kentucky Bourbon
McLain and Kyne	The Wild Turkey	A. Smith Bowman
The Old Pogue	Maker's Mark	

Michael Jackson's Blend

"Michael Jackson was perhaps the most admired whisky writer and taster the world has seen. He traveled relentlessly, seeking out whiskies from far-flung places and brought their flavors to life with unrivalled eloquence. This extremely limited world whisky produced in his honor has been blended from Michael's private collection containing whiskies from many countries and adjusted for balance to produce a very fine dram that we hope he would be proud to drink." *—bottle label, by Alastair Campbell*

WHISKEY FESTIVALS

WhiskyFest (New York, San Francisco and Chicago)
http://www.whiskeyfest.com/

Kentucky Bourbon Festival
http://www.kybourbonfestival.com/

Victoria Whisky Festival
http://www.victoriawhiskyfestival.com/

Spirit of Speyside Whisky Festival
http://www.spiritofspeyside.com/

Scotland's Malt Whisky Trail
http://www.maltwhiskeytrail.com/

FEATURED
INFUSIONS

Here is a selection of some of the best infused drinks from celebrated mixologists across the nation!

THE OYSTER HOUSE

(KATIE LOEB)

The Oyster House is located in Center City, Philadelphia. Owned by the third generation of the Mink family to operate a raw bar in Philadelphia, Oyster House has taken infusions to a whole new level. Head bartender and Mixologist Katie Loeb crafts delectable infusions and serves them in the form of oyster shooters. This, along with house-made Aquavit, complements the raw bar and provides a savory means of combining oysters with a cocktail at the same time.

All of the following drinks by Katie Loeb, Head Mixologist/Bartender, Oyster House, Philadelphia, Pennsylvania

AQUAVIT

This can be served ice cold in small-stemmed cordial glasses, in a Bloody Viking with your favorite Bloody Mary mix, or used as a cocktail ingredient.

2 liters good quality vodka (Katie uses Laird's for this drink)

3 tablespoons caraway seed

2 tablespoons dill seed

2 tablespoons cumin seed

1 tablespoon coriander seed

1 tablespoon fennel seed

2 star anise

3 whole cloves

4 strips each, orange and lemon peel (no pith)

1 ounce demerara sugar syrup, separated

1. Preheat oven to 400°F.

2. Place seeds on a foil-lined cookie sheet or sizzle plate. Toast lightly in the oven for 6-8 minutes, stirring every few minutes until warm and fragrant.

3. Remove and cool slightly. Crush seeds lightly and place into large airtight infusion jar.

4. Add star anise, cloves, citrus peels, and cover with 2 liters of vodka.

5. Seal tightly and shake.

6. Store at room temperature for 2 full weeks. Shake bottle every couple of days to expose the spices again.

7. Strain carefully through fine mesh, chinoise, or a gold coffee filter and rebottle.

8. Add 1 ounce demerara simple syrup and shake well to incorporate.

9. Store in the freezer for best effect.

HORSERADISH VODKA
(NEW ENGLANDER)

1.75 L bottle vodka

2 cups shredded peeled horseradish root

1. Place fresh horseradish in infusion container.
2. Top with full 1.75 L of vodka.
3. Seal tightly and allow to infuse for 24-48 hours.
4. Strain and use with a splash of tomato juice in oyster shooter.

HORSERADISH TEQUILA
(EL CHULO)

1.75 L bottle blanco tequila

2 cups shredded peeled horseradish root

1. Place fresh horseradish in infusion container.
2. Top with full 1.75 L of tequila.
3. Seal tightly and allow to infuse for 24-48 hours.
4. Strain and use with a splash of tomato juice in oyster shooter.

I drink too much. The last time I gave
a urine sample it had an olive in it.

— RODNEY DANGERFIELD

LONDONER

1.75 L gin

2 cups sliced English cucumber, peeled and seeded (half-moons)

Zest of 2 lemons

8 leafy sprigs of dill, bruised

1. Place cucumber, lemon zest, and dill in infusion jar.

2. Top with gin.

3. Allow to infuse 48-72 hours.

4. Strain and use with a small splash of lemon juice in oyster shooter

Better belly burst than
good liquor be lost.

— JONATHAN SWIFT

BANGKOK

1.75 L vodka

½ cup peeled ginger, cut into small disks

2 stalks lemongrass, chopped

¾ cup fresh Thai basil leaves, bruised

1. Place ginger, lemongrass, and Thai basil leaves in infusion jar.
2. Top with vodka.
3. Allow to infuse 48-72 hours.
4. Strain and use with a small splash of lime juice in oyster shooter.

CHIHUAHUA

1.75 L vodka

4 small Thai chili peppers, split and seeds removed (do with gloves)

8 sprigs of cilantro, bruised

1. Place peppers and cilantro in infusion jar.
2. Top with vodka. Allow to infuse 48-72 hours.
3. Strain and use with a splash of tomato juice in oyster shooter.

SERAFIN

1.75 L vodka

4 serrano chili peppers,
split and seeds removed,
cut into rings
(do with gloves)

12 sprigs of tarragon,
bruised

1. Place peppers and tarragon in infusion jar.

2. Top with vodka.

3. Allow to infuse 48-72 hours.

4. Strain and use with a splash of pineapple juice
   in oyster shooter.

Prohibition is better than no liquor at all.

— WILL ROGERS

FRANKLIN MORTGAGE & INVESTMENT CO.

(AL SOTACK)

Franklin Mortgage & Investment Co. is located in Philadelphia, Pennsylvania. The name pays tribute to the art and craftsmanship bartenders brought to the bar in the United States pre-Prohibition era. The name is borrowed from the late 1920s company that ran the biggest underground alcohol ring, even bigger than Al Capone's. They draw from their historical mentors, such as Jerry "The Professor" Thomas, Ada Coleman, and Harry Johnson. Al Sotack, head bartender and infusion creator, serves a drink crafted with precision, care, and expertise.

All the following drinks by Al Sotack, Head Bartender, Franklin Mortgage & Investment Co., Philadelphia, Pennsylvania.

RASPBERRY INFUSED COGNAC

750 ml cognac

½ cup or so raspberries

1. Muddle the raspberries and place in infusion jar.
2. Add cognac and cover for NO MORE THAN 24 HOURS. This infusion works best with tasting between 16 and 24 hours incrementally and pulling when done. You're looking to pull before a sort of "artificial" or metallic flavor sets in.
3. Strain.

WATERMELON AND CILANTRO INFUSED TEQUILA

750 ml blanco tequila

Small watermelon

⅓ bushel cilantro

1. Cut about a dozen 2- to 3-inch cubes of watermelon and add to an infusion jar.

2. Add one-third bushel of cilantro.

3. Add the tequila.

4. Remove cilantro after 15-20 minutes and allow watermelon to sit for 5-7 hours.

5. Strain and serve.

NATIONAL MECHANICS
(PAUL BROWN)

National Mechanics Bar and Restaurant is located in Old City, Philadelphia in a historic building built by William Strickland in 1837. Since then the building has housed banks, churches, and clubs. The bar's name originates from the building's first incarnation, the National Mechanics Bank. With a great mix of old-world feel and new-world charm, bartender Paul Brown entertains his guests with stellar infusions and remarkable cocktails in a laid-back atmosphere.

All of the following drinks by Paul Brown, bartender, National Mechanics, Philadelphia, Pennsylvania.

APPLE WHISKEY

Our Apple Whiskey is made with Canadian Club Whiskey, cinnamon, cloves, vanilla extract, nutmeg, and whichever apples look good this week. For this, we do very little to make this into a Bonita Applebomb. Simply drop 1½ ounces of Apple Whiskey into ½ pint of Smithwick's Irish Ale and throw it back!

I doubt if you can have a truly wild party without liquor.

— CARL SANDBURG

JALAPEÑO TEQUILA

Our jalapeño tequila is made starting with Siembra Azul Blanco Tequila. We add to it, cracked peppercorns and, of course, fresh jalapeños. From this we make a Pineapple Jalapeño Tequila Margarita, which is made with 1 ounce of homemade margarita mix, ½ ounce of pineapple juice, ½ ounce of Combier, and 1½ ounce of our Jalapeño Tequila.

Drinking is a way of ending the day.

— ERNEST HEMINGWAY

BACON VODKA

Our Bacon Vodka is made with filtered vodka, thick bacon cooked lightly, and black pepper. Make sure some of the rendered fat is added to the vodka. We keep the fat in the infusion (it adds to the mystique of the libation), but if you want to take it out, strain it or put in the freezer to solidify the fat. Typically we just add this to Bloody Marys (delicious!) or for the bold, we make a Bacon Chocolate Martini.

Bacon Chocolate Martini

Mix 1 ounce Bacon Vodka with 1 ounce Godiva Chocolate Liqueur. Chill and serve into a martini glass rimmed with chocolate syrup.

Mixologist Q&A
PAUL BROWN

1. How do you decide which flavors (essences) complement which liquors?
The flavors we've used typically come from consideration. Bacon Vodka
was the first as a way to bacon-ize alcohol. Added to neutral vodka allows
only the bacon flavoring to come through. Others we've dealt with have
come up in conversation or just thinking that something may work. There
have been failed experiments....

*2. When you create an infusion do you have a cocktail in mind to use it
in?* When we make an infusion, we don't think too much about its use.
It's alcohol, you can always find a use for it. Often, people (staff, patrons,
anyone) will come up with a drink that (at least they think) is pretty good.
I think the Bacon Vodka Jalapeño Tequila Martini was pretty horrific.

*3. What was the riskiest infusion you tried that ended up coming out
great?* Before the iced tea vodkas became popular, I made a simple
infusion of Lipton tea bags and cane sugar. At first, it was terrible; it had
all of the bitterness and earthiness of tea with nothing else. Given more
time, it had mellowed into a very tasty tincture.

4. Can you give home infusers any tips or advice? If anything I've learned to experiment without being too ambitious all at once. When first making an infusion, keep it simple. You don't want to spend a lot of time just to have it ruined by the third or fourth ingredient. Everything goes into a solution at different times, so there's no knowing what the contribution of several ingredients will be in a week or two.

5. How do you know when an infusion is perfect for serving or bottling? It's easy to know when it's ready because it tastes right. The challenge is sometimes you don't know if it's not ready yet or if it's already past its peak.

6. How long do most infusions take? It depends. For the infusions we use, they're ready in a week. Very bold flavors. If you're doing something subtle (like cucumbers or lemon zest) you'll need more time. It's all part of the fun. My favorite part is remembering something I have started but have forgotten—like this bourbon and cherries that has been sitting around for a year.

I FEEL SORRY for people who don't drink. When they wake up in the morning, that's as good as they're going to feel all day.

— FRANK SINATRA

THE SMOKE JOINT
(JOHN HOFFER)

Owned by Ben Grossman and Craig Samuel, The Smoke Joint is located in Fort Greene, Brooklyn. Along with serving some of the best New York barbeque in a relaxed environment, manager John W. Hoffer offers his patrons some delicious cocktails created from house-made infusions.

All the following drinks by John W. Hoffer, Manager of The Smoke Joint Restaurant Group, The Smoke Joint, Brooklyn, New York.

HABANERO & MANGO TEQUILA

Be careful, this infusion is spicy!

2 bottles of tequila (750 ml)

8 mangoes

1 habanero pepper

1. Peel and slice 8 mangoes and place into the bottom of the infusion jar.

2. Fill infusion jar with tequila.

3. Let infuse for 1 week.

4. Lightly fire roast 1 habanero pepper and place into infusion for 1 day.

5. Open infusion jar and discard the pepper.

6. Pour tequila through a strainer and mash the mango through the strainer into the tequila.

Here's a drink featuring Habanero & Mango Tequila.

Mango Margarita

1. Fill a tumbler with ice.

2. Pour in 2 ounces of Habanero & Mango Tequila and 1 ounce of Cointreau.

3. Fill the tumbler with limonade.

4. Shake, garnish with lime slice, salt the rim of the glass, and serve.

NOTHING IS so musical as the sound of pouring bourbon for the first drink on a Sunday morning. Not Bach or Schubert or any of those masters.

— CARSON MCCULLERS, FROM *CLOCK WITHOUT HANDS*

JALAPEÑO & LIME VODKA

This infused masterpiece is great for the sample cocktails that follow!

2 bottles of vodka (750 ml each)

3 jalapeños

5 limes

1. Take 2 jalapeños and poke holes in them and place them into the bottom of an infusion jar.

2. Take the 1 remaining jalapeño and cut into ½ inch slices and place into infusion jar.

3. Take the 5 limes and cut the ends off and place each lime on end and cut in half, and cut into ½ inch slices and place limes into infusion jar.

4. Empty 2 bottles of vodka into jar.

5. Close infusion jar, date and label.

6. Let sit for 1-2 weeks.

Here they are, the promised recipes featuring
Jalapeño & Lime Vodka.

Smoky Mary

Instructions
1. Add cucumber slice, olive, four squirts of Holla (our house-made hot sauce) or other hot sauce, two squirts of Worcestershire sauce, a heaping bar spoon of horseradish, three shakes of celery salt, six shakes of pepper, and ½ ounce of lemon juice in a mixing glass.
2. Muddle contents and add 2 ounces of Jalapeño & Lime Vodka and 1 can of tomato juice. Shake.
3. Rim tumbler with 78 spice (our house-made rub for BBQ meats) or other BBQ spices.
4. Fill a glass with ice and pour shaken contents into the glass. Garnish with olive on a skewer and a lemon wedge on the rim of the glass.

Trouble Loves Me

1. Add 2 ounces of Jalapeño & Lime Vodka, 1 ounce of triple sec, 1¼ ounces limonade, and ¾ ounce of orange juice to a mixing glass.
2. Shake and strain into a chilled martini glass. Garnish with lime.

SPICED PUMPKIN VODKA

2 bottles vodka
(750 ml bottles)

Small sliced
pumpkin

Cinnamon sugar

½ whole nutmeg

Cinnamon stick

3 cloves

1. Slice a small pumpkin into ½-inch slices and spread out on a sheet pan.

2. Dust the pumpkin slices with cinnamon sugar.

3. Place sheet pan in oven set at 350°F until pumpkin slices begin to brown. Set the sheet pan aside to cool.

4. Place the nutmeg, cinnamon stick, 3 cloves, the cooled off pumpkin slices, and the vodka into an infusion jar and seal.

5. Allow to infuse for 2 weeks.

6. After 2 weeks, strain the vodka, and then place only the pumpkin slices and vodka into blender and blend.

7. After being completely blended, strain the vodka through a strainer to get any large pieces out and now the infusion is ready to serve.

Here's a yummy cocktail featuring Spiced Pumpkin Vodka.

Roasted Pumpkin Spice Cocktail

1. Combine the following ingredients into a chilled cocktail glass: 3 ounces Spiced Pumpkin Vodka, 1½ ounces amaretto, and ½ ounce Baileys.

2. Garnish with toasted pumpkin seeds. (You can use seeds from the pumpkin you used to make the vodka infusion. Wash the seeds, spread them on a sheet pan, dust with cinnamon sugar, and toast them in the oven.)

STRAWBERRY & VANILLA BOURBON

2 bottles (750 ml) bourbon

1 quart of rinsed and sliced strawberries

5 ounces sugar

Vanilla extract

2 whole vanilla beans

1. Hull strawberries and cut them in half.

2. Place strawberries in a bowl and put 5 ounces of vanilla-infused sugar on the top of the strawberries.

3. Place strawberries into the bottom of a clean infusion jar.

4. Cut a slit into both of the vanilla beans and place into the infusion jar.

5. Fill the infusion jar with 2 bottles (750 ml bottles) of bourbon. Close lid.

6. Let infuse for 2 weeks.

Here are a few cocktails featuring Strawberry & Vanilla Bourbon.

Lafayette Limonade

1. Muddle a strawberry at the bottom of a tumbler. Fill with ice.
2. Pour 2 ounces of Strawberry & Vanilla Bourbon over the ice. Fill with limonade, shake, garnish with strawberry and lime, and serve.

Bourbon on Elliott

1. Combine the following ingredients in a tumbler: 1½ ounces Strawberry Bourbon and 1 ounce Malibu.
2. Fill tumbler with orange juice, cranberry, and a splash of grenadine.
3. Fill rocks glass with ice.
4. Shake and pour back into glass. Garnish with a lime wedge.

A drink a day keeps the shrink away.

— EDWARD ABBEY

JOHN W. HOFFER

1. How do you decide which flavors (essences) complement which liquors?
Vodkas are a little more giving as far as flavors to play with. So we have a
wide range of things to try and most end up working nicely. When you put
several ingredients into one infusion, you need flavors that complement
each other. So a little understanding of flavors and an imagination work
well. For bourbon, we choose flavors that already come through a bit in
the bourbons, such as cinnamon, vanilla, as well as cranberries and apples.
For tequila, mango and habanero just popped in my head immediately
and it worked beautifully. The fire-roasted habanero picks up on the light
smokiness of the tequila and the mango plays in perfectly with it.

*2. When you create an infusion do you have a cocktail in mind to use
it in?* I would say the majority of the time my mind starts working on
a cocktail after tasting the finished infusion and we work on it from
there. Sure you have ideas, but it may come out a little differently
than expected.

3. *What was the riskiest infusion you tried that ended up coming out great?* I would have to say the bacon bourbon. We used bacon, brown sugar, and black peppercorns. There is just something strange about bacon floating in a jar full of liquor. It's intriguing for customers to see. That is usually the first one they notice and ask about. Surprisingly everyone who tries it loves it. We are a wonderful BBQ restaurant, so a bacon bourbon fits right in—meat on your plate and smoked meat in your drink.

4. *Can you give home infusers any tips or advice?* Be experimental and you will be surprised by what pairings work. Also, infusions are great holiday and birthday gifts. For restaurants and bars they are a great backdrop for the bar and wonderful conversational pieces.

5. *How do you know when an infusion is perfect for serving or bottling?* It's all about taste. I keep mine on a rotation of two weeks. Sure some can be used before then. But two weeks is what seems to work for the flavors I'm trying to reach and also for the rotation in our establishment.

6. *How long do most infusions last?* Our cocktail menu is based on our infusions, so we burn through them. All the alcohol we infuse with is 80 proof or higher, so the infusions can be kept a long time.

CIENFUEGOS

(JANE DANGER)

Cienfuegos is in the East Village in New York City. Located above the Cuban sandwich shop Carteles, Cienfuegos provides an all-encompassing experience into the port town of Cienfuegos, Cuba, serving all things rum. Mixologist Jane Danger concocts infused rums that are used in matchless cocktails and amazing punches.

All of the following drinks are by Jane Danger, Cienfuegos, New York City, New York.

RUM RAISIN

We use this in a Golden Fizz. We choose Mount Gay Gold because it tastes like a classic choice for imitating the flavor in rum-raisin ice cream. Infuse a liter of the Mount Gay Eclipse Gold and 2½ cups of raisins. Let this set for 24-48 hours. Strain and serve.

ROOIBOS TEA-INFUSED ELIJAH CRAIG 12-YEAR BOURBON

We use this in a punch with lemon and peach brandy. For this one I like how nutty both the tea and bourbon are. Infuse ¼ cup of loose tea leaves in 750 ml of the bourbon. Let it set for twenty minutes, and then strain before drinking.

JANE DANGER

1. How do you decide which flavors (essences) complement which liquors?
I never try to change the overall flavor of a spirit. You want to choose the base spirit that will best display your infusing ingredients.

2. When you create an infusion do you have a cocktail in mind to use it in? Yes. Like for the Rum Raisin, I knew I wanted a dessert style drink, like a Flip or Golden Fizz.

3. What was the riskiest infusion you tried that ended up coming out great? The riskiest infusion I did was probably my silliest—my Jelly Bean Gin, which I did for my Jelly Bean Collins.

4. Can you give home infusers any tips or advice? When home infusing, you should be very careful with teas, herbs, and coffee. Although the quickest to make infusions with, they can become bitter and ruin your infusion very easily. You must time them and taste as you go along to make sure you don't overdo it.

5. *How do you know when an infusion is perfect for serving or bottling?*
I trust my own palate. Timing is always a good start for consistency.

6. *How long do most infusions take?* It depends on what you are infusing and what spirit and strength you chose. Teas, herbs, and dried fruits are very quick. Melons and berries are quick as well. Hard fruits take longer. Chocolate and fatty things such as nuts and bacon need to be chilled and then the fat has to be skimmed off after infusing.

RESOURCES & SUPPLIES

* For oak barrels, glycerin, and other supplies visit these sites:
  http://www.eckraus.com/
  http://www.1000oaksbarrel.com/

* If you want to try a new whiskey but don't feel like shelling out for a whole bottle, check out Drinks by the Dram, a company that offers samples of many fine whiskies.
  http://www.masterofmalt.com/drinks-by-the-dram/

* For whiskey information and supplies, visit Malt Advocate.
  http://www.maltadvocate.com/

* Don't water down your whiskey. Use whiskey stones!
  http://www.thinkgeek.com/caffeine/accessories/ba37/

* An online alcohol-by-volume calculator:
  http://www.cleavebooks.co.uk/scol/ccalcoh4.htm

* Infusion jars:
  http://www.infused-vodka.com/

* Check out these glass-infusion pitchers at Home-Decor.hsn.com:
http://home-decor.hsn.com/colin-cowie-flavor-infusing-glass-pitcher_p-5901466_xp.aspx

* For artificial flavorings for your cordials, check out these retailers:
http://www.shanks.com/
www.lorannoils.com/

* Create your very own ice spheres. Keep your whiskey cold but not watered down with the ice ball mold from Japantrendshop.com:
http://www.japantrendshop.com/ice-ball-mold-for-perfect-ice-spheres-p-244.html

* Have ice spheres delivered directly to your door (for a price) from glace-ice.com:
http://glace-ice.com/

* Create larger ice cubes with items such as a muffin pan available from many outlets including Amazon.com:
http://www.amazon.com/Kitchenaid-Wire-Sled-Muffin-Silicone/dp/B0000DC645/ref=pd_bbs_9?ie=UTF8&s=home-garden&qid=1214605815&sr=8-9

* Sit back and relax with Whisky Magazine.
http://www.whiskymag.com/

GLOSSARY

Alcohol by Volume (AbV): The standard measurement system used to determine the amount of alcohol contained within a total volume of liquid.

Blended Whiskey: Whiskey made from either two or more malt whiskeys or a mixture of grain and malt whiskeys.

Bourbon: Whiskey made in the United States containing, at minimum, 51 percent corn and stored for at least two years in new charred oak barrels. Many bourbon distilleries reside in Kentucky, but it is not a prerequisite for bourbon classification.

Cognac: French brandy.

Cordial: A term used in the Unites states for alcohol containing at least 2.5 percent sugar by weight. Many cordials contain much more than 2.5 percent.

Corn Whiskey: Whiskey that contains a minimum of 80 percent corn that is not required to be aged in wood.

Crème: An alcohol containing milk or cream that should be refrigerated.

Dram: An informal term for a small amount of whiskey.

Decanter: A vessel, often made of crystal, with a matching tight-fitting stopper used to hold liquids. Often used for holding wine or other liquor.

Infusion: The process of flavoring water and liquors with foods, herbs and spices, and other flavorings.

Maceration: An alternate term for infusion, more specifically relating to alcohol.

Malt: Grain that has been allowed to sprout.

Mash: A fermented malt or grain that is used to distill alcohol.

Liqueur: European equivalent term for cordial (used in the United States).

Neat: A bourbon/whiskey drink with nothing added (no ice). Also known as "straight."

Proof: The relative percentage of alcohol to water in a liquor. The origin of the proof measuring system, originally known as "gunpowder proof," came about as a method to "prove" or check the alcoholic content of liquor. Equal parts bourbon and gunpowder were mixed and lit on fire. If the result was a yellow flame, the alcohol was too strong and needed to be further diluted. When an alcohol's flame burned blue, it was known to be "true" and good to drink.

Rye Whiskey: Whiskey made from a minimum of 51 percent rye and matured in new charred oak barrels for at least two years. Rye whiskey must be distilled at less than 80 percent.

Scotch Whiskey: Whisky made in Scotland matured for at least three years and one day in oak casks. Scotch is often (but not always) treated with peat smoke, giving its malt a unique smoky flavor.

Simple Syrup: Sweetening syrup made from equal parts sugar and water.

Single Malt Whiskey: Whiskey made from one source of malted barley from one distillery.

Tennessee Whiskey: Whiskey made in Tennessee and filtered through sugar-maple charcoal.

Vatting/Vated: The process of blending whiskies at home.

Wheat Whiskey: Whiskey made from a minimum of 51 percent wheat. Wheat whiskey is the least common type.

Zest: The outer rind of citrus fruit comprised of the flavorful outer colored portion and the white bitter inner portion.

INDEX

ABOUT CIDER MILL PRESS
BOOK PUBLISHERS

Good ideas ripen with time. From seed to harvest, Cider Mill Press brings fine reading, information, and entertainment together between the covers of its creatively crafted books. Our Cider Mill bears fruit twice a year, publishing a new crop of titles each spring and fall.

Visit us on the Web at
www.cidermillpress.com
or write to us at
12 Port Farm Road
Kennebunkport, Maine 04046